Kathryn Gustafson
Sculpting the Land

by Leah Levy

S P A C E M A K E R   P R E S S

Washington, DC

Cambridge, MA

Front cover:
Entry garden at Shell Petroleum
Rueil-Malmaison, France
Photograph by Kathryn Gustafson

Publisher: James G. Trulove
Art Director: Sarah Vance
Designer: Elizabeth Reifeiss
Editor: Heidi Landecker
Photographer: Luc Boegly, except as noted
Printer: Palace Press, Hong Kong

ISBN 1-888931-06-X

Contents

Acknowledgments

I want to express my gratitude to Kathryn Gustafson for her inspiring work and for the many hours she spent talking about her ideas, answering questions, attending to details, and for responding thoughtfully and with good humor every time.

Peter Walker introduced me to Kathryn Gustafson in 1993, and for his consideration in arranging that first meeting, and his willingness to continue to discuss her work with me, I am especially appreciative. Thank you to Sarah Vance and Liz Reifeiss for creating the fine design in which Gustafson's work can be considered in book form, and to Jim Trulove and Heidi Landecker of Spacemaker Press for assistance with many crucial aspects of the project. I'm grateful to Sandra Harris, Rhonda Killian, Roxanne Holt, Jane Williamson, and Tim Harvey for their help with details throughout the process of writing and producing this book. I am also pleased to acknowledge the photography of Luc Boegly which brings these pages to life with rich images of Gustafson's work.

My heartfelt thank you to Lynne McDonald for her enthusiastic interest in the preparation of the text, and for being first reader; to Dave Barr for exceptional technical assistance; to Noelle Caskey for varied and valuable consultation; to Joy Natoli, garden critic extraordinaire; and most especially to Joel and Kira Fatherree.

Leah Levy
Berkeley, California
1997

To my parents, who through their
example, guided me to a love of gardens,
contemporary art, and nature.
—*Kathryn Gustafson*

For my grandfather, the late milliner
Samuel Goldstein, who shared with me his
passion for ribbon, Paris, and beauty.
—*Leah Levy*

Kathryn Gustafson is an American-born, Paris-educated landscape architect and environmental artist who has been practicing since 1980, primarily in France. Her work pioneers an original vision in landscape architecture, exploring the relationship between her own personally rich esthetic and the public landscapes she creates. Gustafson's projects defy convention in unexpected ways, joining the heroic impulse of the land mover and freeway builder with the graceful elegance of curvaceous sculpting. Rooted in Modernist abstraction, her artistic vocabulary also derives from the elusive qualities of intuition, memory, and emotion. Gustafson's designed landscapes stretch to synthesize the intellectual and the physical with an unanticipated dimension—the psychologically provocative. These works find their context in a balance between historic movements, artistic disciplines, and different countries and cultures.

Gustafson's work has been predominantly civic, institutional, and corporate, including parks, gardens, and community spaces. She addresses the impact of massive infrastructure on the landscape, providing creative solutions to the problem of earth excavated from major engineering projects such as freeways, bridges, tunnels, and reservoirs. Known for her ability to design with these enormous quantities of displaced earth, Gustafson sculpts sensuous landscapes that successfully integrate new infrastructure with its surroundings and the community.

Her brilliance in providing solutions to immense civic problems while making extraordinarily beautiful land sculpture gained attention and respect early in her career. In Morbras, in the Roissy-en-Brie region outside Paris, for example, Gustafson designed a 35-hectare recreational park at the juncture of three communities. The park, which she calls Meeting Point, was completed in 1987 and incorporates more than 300,000 cubic meters of earth excavated in the engineering of a reservoir. Her scheme integrates the reservoir into its natural surroundings with a series of rippling, sculpted planes, offering an artistic solution to the problem of an unearthed landscape.

Similarly, at a site that includes a major freeway interchange connecting the European north-south axis from Holland to France with the east-west axis from Spain through France to Italy, Gustafson conceived a new gateway to the city of Marseilles that incorporates 700,000 cubic meters of earth excavated from a nearby tunnel. For this site, she defined the two large intersecting freeways that create a great "X" with distinct colors and textures, one a green wet zone and the other a buff-colored dry zone. Four triangular areas articulated by the intersection are planted with vibrant red poppies and other field flowers.

Eluding labels and expectations (the work is not Modernist or post-anything), Gustafson aspires to designs that derive from her intuitions about their sites. She believes the memories we carry from our childhood correlate directly to reactions and responses we experience in the landscape and in gardens. Gustafson's own childhood in the desert plateau of the Yakima Valley in Washington provides a source for some of the landscape imagery in her work. Yakima is surrounded by mountains and irrigated by dams built by the U.S. Army Corps of Engineers. Gustafson's vision evokes this background: land movement, water channels, and desert forms contrasted to and interrelated with mountains.

She believes that the more her work is imbued with concept and feeling, the greater its ultimate effect. No matter how massive the scale of a project, it is instilled with qualities that manifest the texture of her own inner life: dynamic shifts in form and plane and flowing, calibrated curves suggestive of sand dunes, the human form, and other less specifically identifiable references.

These characteristics, along with the materials Gustafson selects—water; stone; steel; quantities of manipulated earth; and vegetation, which plays an increasingly greater role in her designs—define both her more contained corporate gardens and her projects of civil engineering scale. Gardens for the headquarters of international corporations, including Shell Petroleum (examined in this book) and Esso/Exxon, both in Rueil-Malmaison outside Paris, and L'Oreal in Aulnay-sous-Bois, all reveal a palette of cascading and undulated mounds of earth, interrupted or delineated by stone emerging from and integrated within the land. In each of these, Gustafson incorporates water as a sculptural element, activating designs and contrasting the rhythmic but static forms of the land. Curved and very defined geometries are also distinctive in Gustafson's work, as is the extreme planar three-dimensionality of her projects.

Kathryn Gustafson at Shell Petroleum

Penne-Mirabeau concept plan

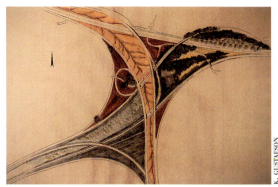

Penne-Mirabeau schematic plan

Detail of model for Penne-Mirabeau freeway exchange and Marseilles gateway

Many architects and landscape architects pay lip service to site responsiveness, but Gustafson strives to address the inherent properties of a site, both in the design possibilities of its physical characteristics and in giving meaning to its resolution. Her process recalls a belief expressed by Simon Schama in *Landscape and Memory*: "Landscapes are culture before they are nature; constructs of the imagination projected onto wood and water and rock."[1] In preparation for a project, Gustafson develops a true relationship with the land, researching its history, developing a deep understanding of its essential qualities and the program for which it is to be designed. In addition, she looks for a rhythm in the land, an element that evokes a memory of her own, allowing her to plumb a broader and more universal unconscious.

The essential quality of Gustafson's Rights of Man Square in Evry, outside Paris (pages 54-63), for example, is its location at the civic heart of a new town. Part of her concept for the square is to emphasize the buildings that surround it by focusing access to them. She parallels this staging of the buildings by creating a stage for the people who populate the plaza as well. At the same time, the design is conceived to isolate and protect, as much as possible, pedestrians from surrounding vehicular traffic.

In the Marseilles gateway and Penne-Mirabeau freeway interchange, Gustafson concentrates on the travel and traffic that reflect the site's key purpose and activity. Two zones of color and texture help travelers distinguish direction, providing a visual and environmental guide. Her design emphasizes the interconnecting and crossing bands of freeway and landscape, visually reiterating and maximizing the specifics of the site.

Gustafson's ability to orchestrate experience on many levels leads to work that engages the senses and also touches aspects of experience that don't easily fall into obvious categories of perception. The sensual qualities of her work afford visitors a heightened overall physical consciousness. Her designs achieve both balance and a slight off-centeredness, awakening an awareness of being in a place that is conceived, planned, and manipulated in the interrelationships of space, form, and evocation of a site's history. (At Evry, for example, the site's history as agricultural fields is evoked by grasslike lines of water that wave in the breeze.) Gustafson's intent

Model for Meeting Point, Morbras, France

Aerial photo of Meeting Point

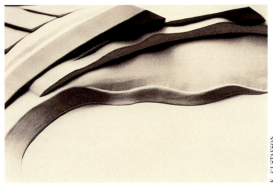

Detail of model, Meeting Point beach area

Aerial photo of Meeting Point

is to register a response among those who visit her landscapes, even to slightly disturb, at least at first. To do so, she employs elements that surprise, like the walls that emerge from the rolling berms she designed for Shell Petroleum's corporate headquarters (pages 42-53) or the unexpected scale of the grand staircase at Evry.

Gustafson's work also evokes a sense of wonder and beauty usually summoned by more traditional landscapes, whether natural or designed. Her multifaceted gardens unfold in sequence, providing time and space for encountering each element individually, in relationship to one another, and to the whole. Whether or not people experiencing Gustafson's work are aware of her underlying ideas, her intention is that they sense those ideas, perhaps unconsciously. This connection—the way the landscapes "become a part of one's body"—is key to the strength of her work.

Gustafson also makes profound associations between our internal experiences and the external landscapes she designs. This intimacy, coupled with her extraordinary sense of the panoramic and epic stance of the work, gives projects such as the Morbras reservoir an accentuated sense of scale. Although the project is very large, Gustafson's attention to the waves and shifts of land at the reservoir's edges; the undulated grades in the landscape that surrounds it; and especially the ribbons of grassy, rolling planes clustered around the reservoir's north shore create a delicate, almost jewel-like form. The massiveness of the space and the conscious resolution of detailing typical of more intimate spaces blend beautifully in these designs.

The boldness of Gustafson's work is predicated by her quiet, ardent energy. She is an intensely private person, who overcomes a powerful shyness to achieve a forceful voice in her landscapes. Her method of working is that of the artist forging emotion and concept into form in an isolated studio. After she has conducted library research, site visits, and interviews with users and clients, she begins a profoundly introspective design process. She starts by listing words that evoke existing or desired meanings, feelings, ambiances, and then expresses these with sketched images that often relate to the landscape and the human form. These early drawings are the foundation for three-dimensional clay models, a fluid and tactile transposition of her thoughts into abstract forms. From the clay, she casts rubber molds, then pours plaster into them, creating miniature models of the landscapes she intends to fashion.

This personal, intuitive process may seem incongruous for one who is also exceptionally open to collaboration and responsive to her clients' needs. But Gustafson must find her own way through a project first. Moving away from logic and control, she makes this journey in a kind of creative free fall. "I want my work to provide a window into a different reality for people," Gustafson explains. "My hope is that my intuitive method of working manifests so that people will connect viscerally with the work in a way that makes it their own, provides a lens for their own vision. I cannot define what that will be exactly. Each person has an individual response." Believing that feelings carry energy, she empowers her art, charging it with her own expression, which transforms into others' direct experiences, a kind of garden alchemy.

Gustafson was born in 1951 in Yakima, Washington, where she lived until she left for the University of Washington in Seattle at 18, and then for New York City at 19 to study at the Fashion Institute of Technology. There, working with fabric

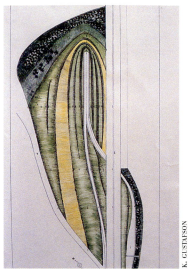

Master plan for Breast Plate, tunnel entrance near Paris, unbuilt

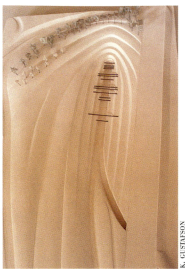

Detail of model for Breast Plate

and textiles, her fascination with the possibilities of fluidity of line, form, and dimension found expression in the techniques of fabric draping. Working in both New York City and Paris for much of the 1970s as a fashion designer, she felt a great affinity with the French sensibility and began to study the language in 1975, the year she made Paris her primary home.

Attracted by the possibility of designing larger-scale works with more permanence, Gustafson decided to study landscape architecture at the premiere French landscape school, the Ecole Nationale Supérieure du Paysage at Versailles, in 1977. She opened her own office in Paris in 1980. Conceptually and literally, her landscapes are a continuum from her earlier work with textiles, evidenced by the organic forms that inspire her projects.

She admires an eclectic selection of artists and designers: Isamu Noguchi, Agnes Martin, Kasmir Malevich, Wassily Kandinsky, Antonio Gaudí, Dennis Oppenheim, Richard Tuttle, Willem de Kooning. Her sources reveal a blending of organic and spiritual expression with a commitment to unified form and meaning. These qualities emerged in Gustafson's own work on the land at a time that

coincided historically with a remarkable moment in artistic culture, the transition from Modernism and Minimalism to what has been termed a postmodern and postminimal period.

Gustafson's decision in the 1970s to abandon textile design for a larger and more public scale occurred at a time when artists such as Michael Heizer, Mary Miss, Robert Smithson, James Turrell, and Richard Long were venturing into sitespecific installations and open-space works. The late 1970s generated another group of artists, primarily women, who distinguished themselves with land art that fused abstract form and cultural meaning. Artists such as Michelle Stuart, Ana Mendieta, Alan Saret, and Jackie Ferrara broke with an essentially formalistic approach to include references that were subjective, anthropomorphic, and psychological.[2] Although Gustafson didn't know these artists personally, their work and hers represent the beginning of a less formal, more evocative approach to the art of landscape design that continues to influence both artists and design professionals.

The late 1970s were also a crucial transitional period in architecture and landscape architecture. Eschewing the

philosophical and practical polarities of the time—design versus ecology, form versus livability, art versus craft—Gustafson committed herself to functional designs that integrate beauty and livability. She delved into the issues that excited her the most: discovering how to retain a work's subjectivity despite its public forum, achieving the skills to build projects in massive scale, and learning to work with engineers and construction teams to orchestrate the huge building projects her designs became. Yet to be resolved was the issue of an audience sufficiently committed to the art of landscape to commission her work and maintain it once it was built.

That audience was clearly French. Culturally and traditionally dedicated to the value of the art of garden design and the rigors of maintenance, and with its own powerful history of Modern gardens,[3] French society experienced a burgeoning economic growth in the 1980s that led to significant new construction. Open to esthetically meaningful landscapes, the French have also long been attracted to the sometimes fantastic implications of surrealism, a clearly sensual undertone in Gustafson's work. Beginning in 1983 with the landscape design for the south glass facade (by the Paris architecture and engineering group RFR—Peter Rice, Martin Francis, and Ian Ritchie) of the Museum of Science and Industry in Parc de la Villette in Paris, French civic and national officials patronized her work with an enthusiasm that has yet to be matched in her own country. Among the dozens of projects she has completed in France, major works include Meeting Point recreational park (1987); Shell Petroleum headquarters and Rights of Man Square (both completed in 1991); the L'Oreal headquarters, with its 1.5-hectare garden with spiraling canals and mounds of earth (1992); the Esso/Exxon headquarters, where a series of rolling and stepped hills is interspersed with a linear pattern of stone canals (1992); the Marseilles gateway, a 30-hectare landscape that incorporates sculptural land forms and lighting (1994); a project to create high-tension pylons for Electricité de France with Ian Ritchie and RFR(1995); and Imaginary Garden, an 8-hectare park overlooking the historic village of Terrasson-la-Villedieu in the Dordogne region (1996). Significant projects outside France begun in 1997 include a major transformation of Crystal Palace Park, London, with John Lyall

Architects and Baxters Engineering; design of a 14-hectare landscape for Western Park Gasfabriek, Amsterdam, with Mecanoo Architects; and a temporary sound and wind garden for the city of Lausanne, Switzerland.

Since 1993, Gustafson has maintained studios in both France and the United States, dividing her time equally between Paris and Vashon Island, just off the Washington State coast near Seattle.

Ultimately, Gustafson's discipline is sculpting and the land is her medium. She shapes the ground plane, as if to forestall nature's whims and repair previous cultural disruption by embedding her own designed forms in the landscape. In changing the surface form of the earth itself, she "moves the earth," literally and figuratively, under a visitor's feet, actively altering the physical relationship between the space and the person in it. What people experience and remember most profoundly about her designed spaces is their sensual quality. Gustafson's rolling lawns and garden floors, the changing levels of her plazas and squares, are a three-dimensional mark on what is most often a two-dimensional plane.

Model for Esso/Exxon headquarters near Paris

K. GUSTAFSON

Model for Thames Barrier Park,
London, competition entry

12

Gustafson also alters the land with water: fountains spring forth directly from the floor of a plaza, as if magically spouting from stone; pools and basins shimmer and funnel in a complex choreography; cascading waterfalls defy a visitor's ability to identify their sources; and sculptural elements are formed by or filled with water, tinted with glistening hues from natural and artificial light.

She employs lighting in landscape to accentuate form, whether natural, or structural. Underscoring the effects of reflected light, her work explores the way we experience natural light in degrees, depending on the angle of the sun or, at night, the phase of the moon. Emphasizing light's mysterious character, the work often hides or integrates light sources, employing fountains, walls, or masts as illumination devices. Light makes rhythmic patterns, shoots across surfaces in bands, and moves through water in ever-changing motifs.

Gustafson's work contains a dichotomy of the bucolic and the unexpected. Her beautiful landscapes have an otherworldly edge, affording a sense of both the natural and the unnatural. The refined massiveness of her work, a Herculean fearlessness that incorporates

the moving of great hunks of earth and stone to create something quite delicate and arresting in its beauty, offers an experience both whimsical and profound. Her strong commitment to functional and practical designs drives her to produce evocative landscapes that also work exceedingly well within their mandate. Since her images and forms originate from an intuition, a sketch, and a clay model, the effort and skill required to realize a final version in massive, three-dimensional granite, for instance, reveal her extraordinary ability to translate ideas into technically achieved realities. Indeed, her reputation for being able to successfully build the projects she imagines continues to grow, a fact that is enticing new clients internationally from both the corporate and public realms.

She tackles spaces and problems with boldness, partnering her personal iconography of memory and feeling with very public, often vast spaces. Without overcrowding or compacting, she fills sites with a rich variety of complementary elements. Leaving little to chance, she sees each artistic and technical challenge as an opportunity to make something interesting and useful, resulting in multileveled work

that is subtle in its revelation and powerful in its effect. Over time, a visitor to a Gustafson landscape begins to sense the master planning behind even the smallest detail, and to appreciate the total environmental experience that such careful planning provides.

Gustafson employs scale to convey the epic, unfolding nature and sequence of her designs. Formed as journeys of discovery, her landscapes are a series of shapes and sculpturally treated forms, orchestrated and exaggerated to emphasize visitors' collective experience. People move through her work like Alice through Wonderland, altering perceptions of their own positions in an ever-changing environment. Magnifying the reality of our living world, Kathryn Gustafson lures us to peer into a Narcissus-like mirror that reflects how we truly exist and participate within the natural world.

Shell Petroleum

Rueil-Malmaison, France

Rights of Man Square

Evry, France

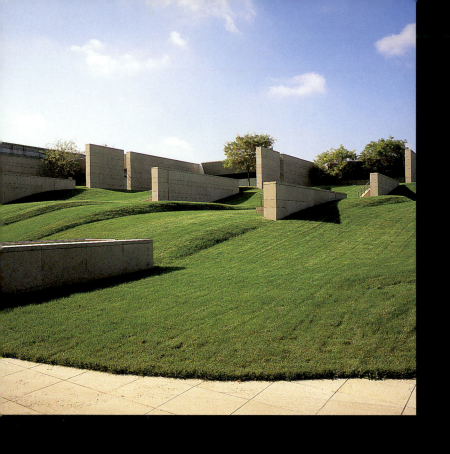
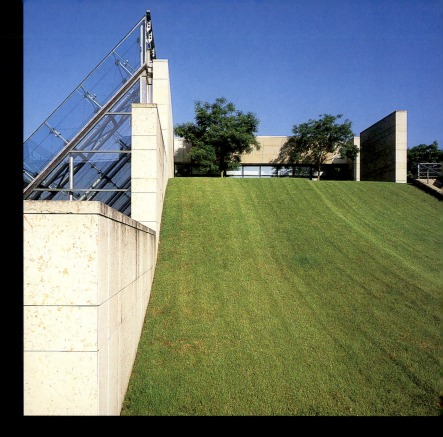
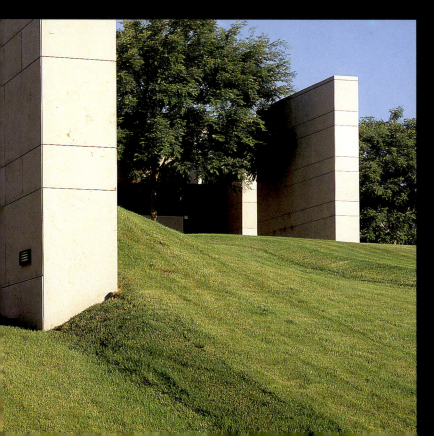

42   Shell Petroleum

Rueil-Malmaison, France

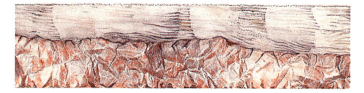

"Fossil stone" drawings by Kathryn Gustafson

Client: *Shell Petroleum*
Landscape team: *Kathryn Gustafson*
                    landscape architect
                    Melissa Brown, project architect
                    Natalie Boyce, Karl Brugmann,
                    Sylvie Farges, project team
Architect: *Valode and Pistre*
Engineer: *Serete Constructions*
Contractors: *GTM-BTP/Quillery, structural*
                    Rossi, vertical stone and granite
                    France Sol, horizontal stone
                    Saunier Duval, lighting
                    CGEE Dolbeau, fountain systems
                    ETM Voisin, metalworks
                    Moser, landscape

"Fossil stones" were fabricated by stone carver who replicated Gustafson's model

Exterior fencing during construction

Entry garden during construction

Echoing the work of Shell Petroleum, which extracts fossil fuels from the ground to "create comfort through energy," Kathryn Gustafson's concept for the gardens at Shell Petroleum's new headquarters in Rueil-Malmaison, 19 kilometers outside Paris, originated from sketches of natural forms rising from beneath the earth. Gustafson expressed the notion of forces moving up and out of the earth in a vocabulary of emerging stones and sinuous waves. Obvious affinities for images that "ribbon" can be traced to her work with fabrics but also find root in her experiences in the desert during a visit to Egypt and to archetypical shapes, including those of the human body. To Gustafson, these representations symbolize reaching out into the world, scanning to the end of literal sight to imagined vistas, stretching the mind to its farthest range.

Having outgrown a location near the Champs Elysées in Paris, Shell wanted its new 2.5-hectare suburban complex near the Seine to be stimulating and beautiful, luring employees away from the heart of the city. The architecture, designed by the French firm of Valode and Pistre, arranges administrative offices in four parallel blocks linked to a single winged volume of subsidiary offices to the east. These office blocks border a large entry plaza and personnel services building in the northwest quadrant of the site.

The office buildings are composed primarily of granite and limestone, juxtaposed with dramatic walls of glass. A ground-floor glass gallery suggests an elegant greenhouse offering views to the various garden spaces that surround it. The personnel building, for the company's more than 2,000 employees, includes conference rooms, a medical facility, and shipping and eating areas, and connects to the main structure by three glazed bridges traversing an aquatic garden. The plan of Shell's new headquarters is designed to encourage movement between the buildings, and the gardens are designed to engage the occupants at every turn.

Inspiration for the landscape and gardens at Shell was generated not only by the architecture and the theme of emerging forms but also by Gustafson's own careful study of the structure of the company, the site, and its surrounding community. Her perception of Shell as a large international corporation that maintains an image of solidity, innovation, and strength guided her elegant, powerful design. She also sought to convey the company's mandate to address key environmental issues relevant to energy production. While Gustafson's gardens do not present political points of view, they literally and metaphorically reflect some of the issues Shell faces in today's cultural and scientific climate.

This expression finds form in varied themes and materials, in juxtapositions of coolness and lushness, hardness and softness, and neutral and vibrant colors that keep interrelationships active and sometimes surprising. Changes of scale, color, visual focus, and stroke (from very broad to very detailed) represent a journey of experiences, rich in movement, one leading into another, with transitions arranged to form a remarkable progression.

The Shell Petroleum landscape has three main spaces, each designed to emulate, in relative scale, a component of the company's relationship to the international community, its own corporate community, and the individual.

A grand 10,000-square-meter entry garden, whose scale refers to the company's international scope, comprises the largest segment of the Shell landscape plan and includes three distinct elements: an elongated, rectangular pool to the east; a wide limestone entry walkway that runs north-south; and a series of dramatically undulated grassy knolls to the west. A 15-by-150-meter aquatic garden, whose scale reflects the more immediate community of those who work at Shell, is traversed daily by everyone at the site via enclosed walkways. In Gustafson's conception, the aquatic garden expresses the relationship of Shell to the people whose lives are enhanced by the company's products. Finally, six smaller, distinctly monochromatic "pocket" gardens are located in private areas behind the office wings and are designed to be viewed from above. The small gardens change with the seasons, animating views from individual offices.

Visitors and employees approach the Shell complex through a narrow residential street in a neighborhood of compact postwar houses, each with its own idiosyncratic character and small, well-kept garden. In this cozy residential environment, arrival at a corporate headquarters comes as something of a surprise. At the end of the street, a visitor comes upon a rolling parklike lawn, with a simple steel fence set back in graduated increments from where grass and sidewalk meet. The receding

Twelve-meter-high stainless steel light mast

Building and sunscreen integrated with yellow pocket garden

Model of Shell Petroleum headquarters

fence affords a sense of access and inclusion. This unusually sensitive transition from residential neighborhood to corporate headquarters ultimately gives way to a limestone wall, where an eye-level slit allows a first glimpse inside the Shell site. A modest gate with a buzzer marks the actual entrance.

The spacious limestone entry plaza at the north side of the complex offers a rather formal introduction to the Shell property. On a low stone wall, an unadorned metal bas-relief of Shell Petroleum's well-known symbol greets visitors, announcing both the company and its elegant building and gardens.

To the east, a 110-meter-long recti-linear pool extends the length of the plaza and escorts visitors to the front door of a glazed lobby rotunda. The plaza rises progressively as it approaches the entrance of the building, so that water in the pool is above the walkway near the gate and just below the walkway near the entrance, appearing to shift with the plaza's geometry. This gesture begins the thread of shifting ground planes that is reiterated throughout the complex.

Four 12-meter-high, 60-centimeter-diameter stainless steel light masts with spiral tops are placed at equal intervals within the pool itself. These masts, symbolizing beacons of light and energy, represent Shell's oil refining and energy production work. The masts also balance the relationship of the landscape and the architecture, physically and metaphorically. They are reflected in the surface of the building, creating a shimmering dupli-cate image, and are aligned with a series of ginkgo trees planted along the pool and walkway's north-south axis. Gustafson's repetition of images and themes in archi-tectural and natural objects is one of the encompassing experiences of Shell.

Along the eastern edge of the pool, a low weir of marble-like Brazilian green granite forms a waterfall causing the pro-gressively louder sound of cascading water as a visitor approaches the building entrance. The water mediates between the white coolness of the limestone walk-way and the rich waves of grass of the garden to the west.

The dramatic fluctuations of these berms form one of the most spectacular elements of the Shell design. This 70-by-80-meter lawn of thick grass turf arranged in rolling forms offers a luxurious sense of movement. Gustafson counterpoints the

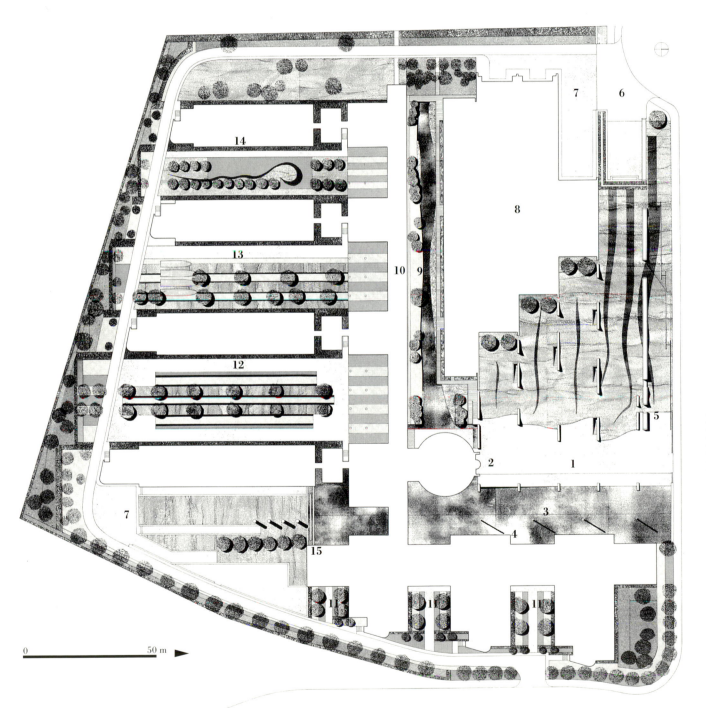

1   Entry plaza
2   Building entry
3   Entry pool
4   Stainless steel light masts
5   Underground parking ventilation
6   Parking garage entrance
7   Service bay
8   Personnel services building
9   Aquatic garden
10 Glass-enclosed gallery corridor
11 Blue pocket garden
12 White pocket garden
13 Yellow pocket garden
14 Red pocket garden with
    inverted question mark
15 Waterfall

0   50 m

Tree planting in aquatic garden during construction

Yellow pocket garden

Red pocket garden with inverted question mark

46   lyrical rhythms with hard-edged limestone walls that seem to emerge from the grass-carpeted mounds. The juxtaposition of these French-quarried walls and swelling hills suggests many possible references: the curved rooftops and angled chimneys of historic Paris architecture, ocean waves and geometric ships, the arcs and hard angles found in traditionally manicured French parks.

Gustafson designs landscapes for people to move through, defining a baseline as departure and checkpoint. She shifts views, angles, and perspectives to provide new experiences of a space, akin to walking in a sculpture and seeing it anew from every angle. At Shell, the wall sections have an anthropomorphic movement, emerging from beneath the rolling lawn and progressing across the limestone walkway to the pool, metaphors for water seeking its own level, or a kind of surrealistic "school" of walls "swimming" across the landscape.

As they ascend at different heights from beneath the earth, the walls hint at earth energy, a recurring theme in Gustafson's work. They also allude to the fluidity of oil emerging and ultimately powering the world above. These walls,

while crafted at specific heights and shapes integral to the design, also house certain functional necessities: fire escapes, emergency smoke ventilation systems for four underground parking lots, and a service entry are arranged where the walls surface. An office building, part of Shell's services facility, lies under these hills and walls; the technical feat of crafting this landscape atop a functioning workplace is a tribute to both Gustafson's engineering instincts and her exceptional focus on detail.

Rectangular stones from both the lawn and the pool protrude along the entry walkway. These limestone elements suggest metamorphosis: those emerging from the pool have a rough surface texture, while those emerging from the lawn are smooth.

Visitors arriving from the street follow the path of the entry plaza walkway, but others, including those working at Shell, park in a garage beneath the complex and ascend into a lobby rotunda on the south side of the entry plaza. Here they are greeted by a view of the aquatic garden, a multilayered, heavily planted area that focuses on a long, ribbonlike waterway extending metaphorically to the Seine, about 500 meters beyond. People

at Shell call it the Impressionist Garden, a nod to the lush colors of its varied vegetation and to the nearby Ile du Chatou, a favorite painting site for the French Impressionists, whose famous proximity is part of the culture of the region.

Throughout the Shell gardens and in a number of other projects, Gustafson employs the ribbon as a metaphor for life: moving up and down, ebbing and flowing, as life and nature do. Ribbons shine, so the reality and illusion of fading and reflecting light are reprises not only in the shapes and forms of Gustafson's work, but also on the surfaces. She incorporates water or polished stone, reflective surfaces that create permutations at every turn. Others working with a parallel concentration on beauty and sensuous curves might be considered romantic, facile, or one-dimensional, but Gustafson's ability to evoke the shadow keeps the work far from sentimental or simplistic, pushing it to the realm of mystery and intensity.

A swath of raised earth abuts the straight edge of the building on one side and the curving aquatic garden on the other. Richly planted with dogwood, magnolia, rhododendron, and azalea, the flower patterns in this swath contain a

rainbow of colors from white to purple, repeating colors central to other gardens in the project. Iroko, a cultivated exotic hardwood, aligns the rippled edge of the garden bed, so that the play of water, flowers, and trees complements the building's hard edges with variation and texture.

A 1.5-meter-wide by 120-meter-long walkway hovers above the water, providing intimate access to the aquatic garden. Made of wood slats with stainless steel supports, the walkway echoes with the sound of footsteps as one moves along. Leaning over the railing, visitors and employees can peer into the water, taking in the varied gardens and surrounding buildings. This phenomenon of being at the center of so many perspectives at once makes a kind of magical experience, far beyond what one might expect of a corporate headquarters. The walkway's only destination is into the heart of the garden; it is a device designed to pull visitors into the scheme, dropping a person, as it were, into the middle of a grand garden maze, orchestrating an opportunity to become lost in the environment. The garden offers this meditative encounter in a Zen-like setting for contemplating the sound of the water but also suggests the experience of walking a jungle path engulfed by dense, rich vegetation.

Night lighting at entry

Aquatic garden

Aquatic garden

47

The aquatic garden is memorable in the tradition of the grand parks and gardens of France. With all its components, the space allows the visitor, even when standing on the walkway in the middle of the garden, to experience each aspect individually as well as in integrated relation to the others.

Along one side of the aquatic garden, Valode and Pistre's extraordinary wall of inclined glass recalls a greenhouse. Echoing its materials and volume, three glazed bridges traverse the garden to link offices with the cafeteria and other employee amenities.

Visible from the rotunda, the entrance and aquatic garden are available to the public, visitors, and Shell employees. To the south as well as behind the subsidiary office wing are a series of elongated pocket or private gardens, each with its own theme, designed more to be seen from offices than to be visited. Each pocket garden incorporates a selection of plants that reflects one of the colors from other parts of the plan.

A yellow pocket garden, for example, uses buttercup ivy and bright yellow-flowering and yellow-leaved trees trimmed to reach upward rather than outward. A white garden, composed of white iceberg roses and *Artemisia schmidtiana*, is planted in parallel linear beds.

A red pocket garden, incorporating flowering cherry trees, is positioned below the administrative offices. Its red roses are arranged in a reversed question mark—Gustafson's suggestion to Shell's executives that they continually ponder whether they are asking themselves the right questions.

Each pocket garden is framed by a trimmed evergreen hedge that creates the effect of a series of tapestries. The entire landscape is also framed with a variety of shrubs that provide privacy for both Shell and its neighbors and a formal delineated edge to the design.

Since darkness falls early during French winters, Gustafson incorporated lighting throughout the Shell gardens to extend the experience of the outside into the interior of the building. Lights at the tops of the spiral masts emphasize their height, lights along the base of the walls that emerge from the rolling knolls elaborate their volume and mass, and the changing pattern and reflections produced by lighting from within the water enliven the pools. The entry walkway is illuminated at night with softly focused lamps, so that one's way is effectively lit, but the rest of the garden is seen through the contrasts of shadow and light.

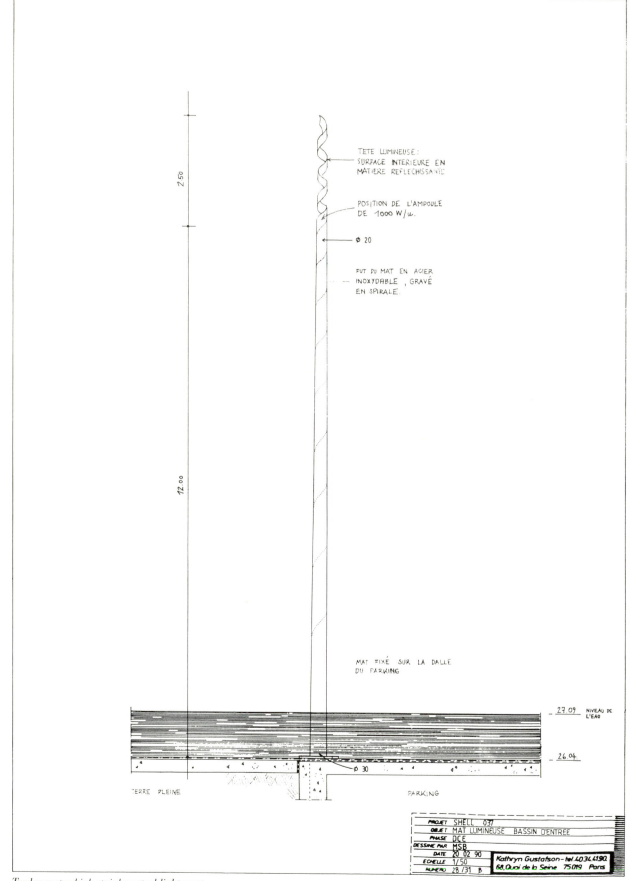

TETE LUMINEUSE:
SURFACE INTERIEURE EN
MATIERE REFLECHISSANTE

POSITION DE L'AMPOULE
DE 1000 W/u.

Ø 20

FUT DU MAT EN ACIER
INOXYDABLE, GRAVÉ
EN SPIRALE.

2.50

12.00

MAT FIXÉ SUR LA DALLE
DU PARKING

27.09   NIVEAU DE
        L'EAU

26.04

Ø 30

TERRE PLEINE

PARKING

PROJET	SHELL 037
OBJET	MAT LUMINEUSE BASSIN D'ENTREE
PHASE	DCE
DESSINE PAR	MSB
DATE	20 02 90
ECHELLE	1/50
NUMERO	28 /31 B

Kathryn Gustafson - tel. 40.34.41.90.
68, Quai de la Seine 75.019 Paris

Twelve-meter-high stainless steel light mast

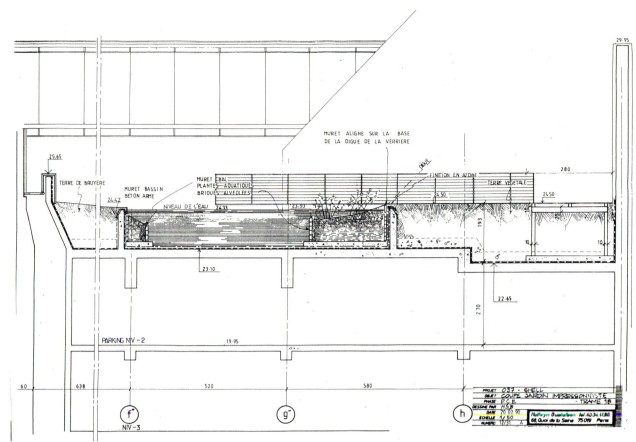

Section of aquatic garden over underground parking garage 49

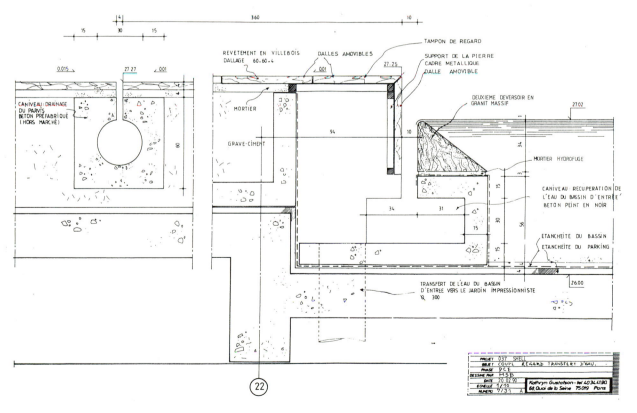

Section of entry walkway and pool with granite weir

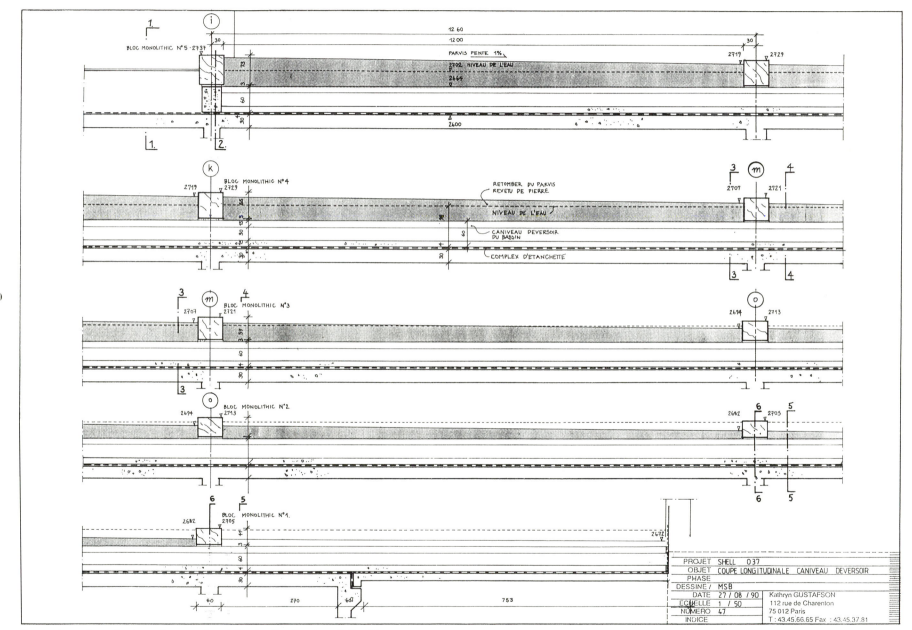

Progressive sections of entry walkway and pool showing the changing relationship
between the water and the walkway

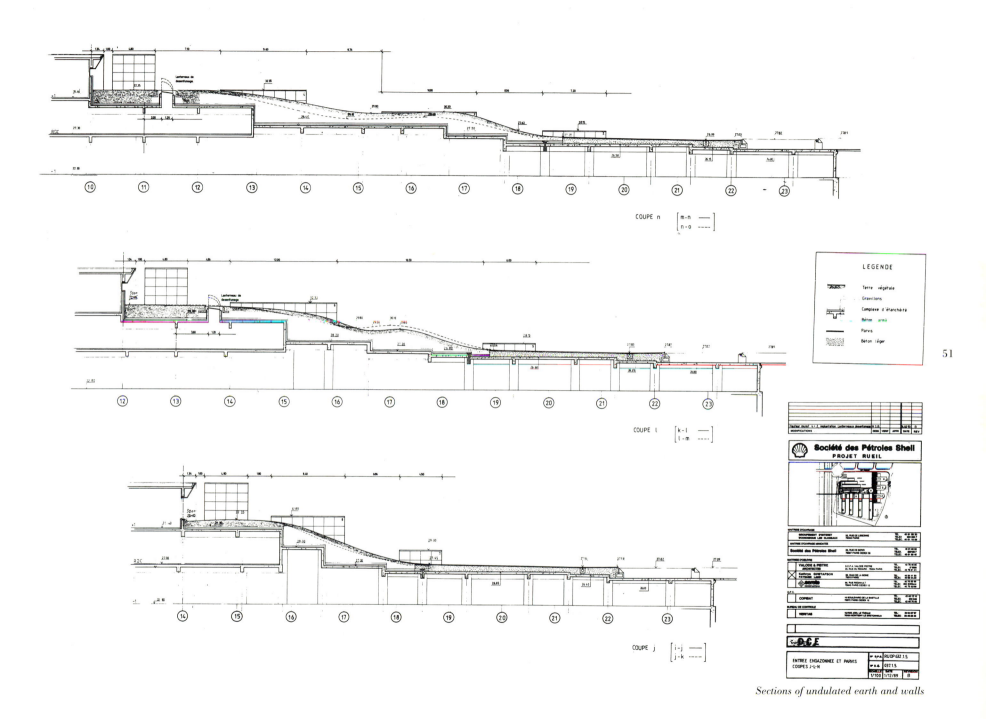

COUPE n [m-n ———]
         [n-o -----]

COUPE l [k-l ———]
         [l-m -----]

COUPE j [i-j ———]
         [j-k -----]

LEGENDE

Terre végétale
Gravillons
Complexe d'étanchéité
Béton armé
Parvis
Béton léger

51

ENTREE ENGAZONNEE ET PARVIS
COUPES J-L-N

Société des Pétroles Shell
PROJET RUEIL

Sections of undulated earth and walls

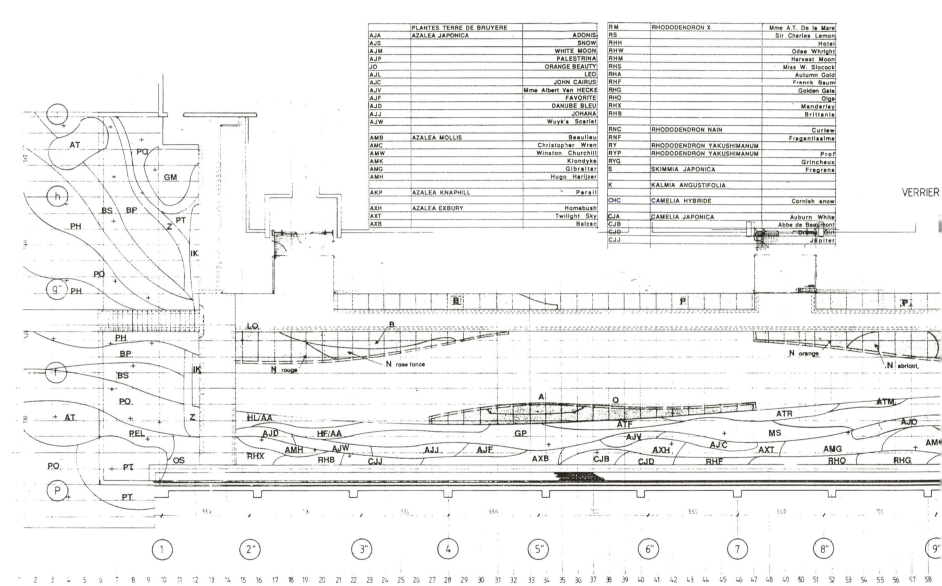

	PLANTES TERRE DE BRUYERE	
AJA	AZALEA JAPONICA	ADONIS
AJS		SNOW
AJM		WHITE MOON
AJP		PALESTRINA
JO		ORANGE BEAUTY
AJL		LEO
AJC		JOHN CAIRUS
AJV		Mme Albert Van HECKE
AJF		FAVORITE
AJD		DANUBE BLEU
AJJ		JOHANA
AJW		Wuyk's Scarlet
AMB	AZALEA MOLLIS	Beaulieu
AMC		Christopher Wren
AMW		Winston Churchill
AMK		Klondyke
AMG		Gibraltar
AMH		Hugo Harijzer
AKP	AZALEA KNAPHILL	Persil
AXH	AZALEA EXBURY	Homebush
AXT		Twilight Sky
AXB		Balzac

RM	RHODODENDRON X	Mme A.T. De la Mare
RS		Sir Charles Lemon
RHH		Hotei
RHW		Odee Whright
RHM		Harvest Moon
RHS		Miss W. Slocock
RHA		Autumn Gold
RHF		Franck Baum
RHG		Golden Gate
RHO		Olga
RHX		Manderlay
RHB		Brittania
RNC	RHODODENDRON NAIN	Curlew
RNF		Fragantissima
RY	RHODODENDRON YAKUSHIMANUM	
RYP	RHODODENDRON YAKUSHIMANUM	Prof
RYG		Grincheux
S	SKIMMIA JAPONICA	Fragrans
K	KALMIA ANGUSTIFOLIA	
CHC	CAMELIA HYBRIDE	Cornish snow
CJA	CAMELIA JAPONICA	Auburn White
CJB		Abbe de Beaumont
CJD		Drama Girl
CJJ		Jupiter

VERRIER

Planting plan for Impressionist Garden

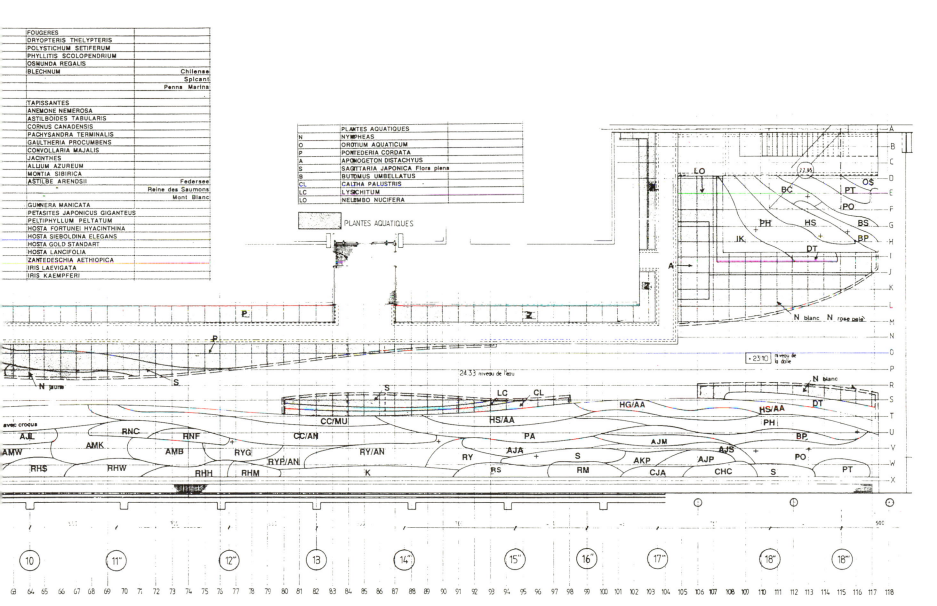

FOUGERES	
DRYOPTERIS THELYPTERIS	
POLYSTICHUM SETIFERUM	
PHYLLITIS SCOLOPENDRIUM	
OSMUNDA REGALIS	
BLECHNUM	Chilense
	Spicant
	Penna Marina
TAPISSANTES	
ANEMONE NEMEROSA	
ASTILBOIDES TABULARIS	
CORNUS CANADENSIS	
PACHYSANDRA TERMINALIS	
GAULTHERIA PROCUMBENS	
CONVOLLARIA MAJALIS	
JACINTHES	
ALLIUM AZUREUM	
MONTIA SIBIRICA	
ASTILBE ARENDSII	Federsee
	Reine des Saumons
	Mont Blanc
GUNNERA MANICATA	
PETASITES JAPONICUS GIGANTEUS	
PELTIPHYLLUM PELTATUM	
HOSTA FORTUNEI HYACINTHINA	
HOSTA SIEBOLDINA ELEGANS	
HOSTA GOLD STANDART	
HOSTA LANCIFOLIA	
ZANTEDESCHIA AETHIOPICA	
IRIS LAEVIGATA	
IRIS KAEMPFERI	

	PLANTES AQUATIQUES	
N	NYMPHEAS	
O	OROTIUM AQUATICUM	
P	PONTEDERIA CORDATA	
A	APONOGETON DISTACHYUS	
S	SAGITTARIA JAPONICA Flora plena	
B	BUTOMUS UMBELLATUS	
CL	CALTHA PALUSTRIS	
LC	LYSICHITUM	
LO	NELUMBO NUCIFERA	

PLANTES AQUATIQUES

53

54 **Rights of Man Square**

Evry, France

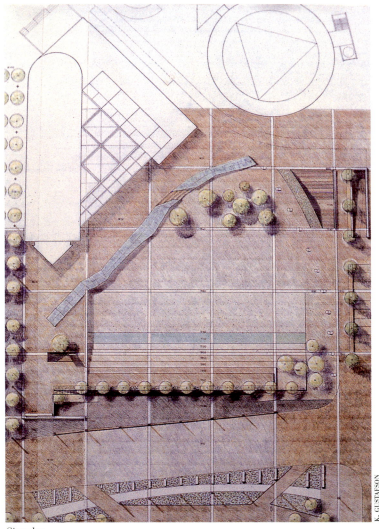

Site plan

K. GUSTAFSON

Client: *City of Evry*
Landscape team: *Kathryn Gustafson*
     landscape architect
     Gérard Pras, project architect
     Caroline Barthelmebs, Sylvie
     Farges, project team
Engineers: *Sectec TPI, Jean Paul Bonroy*
Contractors: *Chantier Moderns, underground*
     parking and basin structure
     Traveaux Routier, paving, metal,
     lighting, and landscape
     CGEE Dolbeau, fountains

View from top of cathedral

View looking west

Vehicle entry to underground parking

Evry is one of five new towns created in the 1970s outside Paris to decentralize the overcrowded French capital. Located 21 kilometers southeast of Paris, and only 15 minutes by train from the center of the city, Evry outgrew its original town hall and city center in the late 1980s when the population reached 80,000. Cooperating federal, regional, and local governmental agencies assigned to monitor the expansion of Evry solicited three proposals for a unifying plaza at the heart of the new town center expansion. Kathryn Gustafson, collaborating with architect Gérard Pras, was chosen in 1989 to design the plaza.

The competition organizers established the plaza's theme as the Rights of Man, part of the French constitution essentially comparable to the U.S. Bill of Rights. Gustafson took her inspiration from the Rights of Man's Article Number 11, freedom of expression. She conceived of the square as a space for private and public expression, encompassing civic gatherings, individual oratory, and cultural programs including dance, theater, and music performances. Her scheme offered a dynamic background for these cultural activities, an inviting plaza where locals might eat lunch or meet a friend, and a park of arche-

typical amenities recalling the countryside: the sound of water, the sense of the wind blowing across fields. Gustafson envisioned a plaza that would elevate everyday experiences to the level of art and also provide a civic heart for a community whose own history was limited to a few decades.

Rights of Man Square is surrounded by Evry's busy infrastructure, including a train station, urban streets, and parking garages. The square is bordered on the north by the national highway that runs from Paris to the south of France. New institutional buildings by internationally recognized architects dominate the periphery of the plaza, recalling the configuration of medieval town squares. These bordering structures include the Chamber of Commerce and Industry by Philippe and Martine Deslandes to the east; a town hall by Jacques Levy on the south side; and, to the southwest, Saint Corbinien Cathedral of the Resurrection and its cloister by the Swiss-Italian architect Mario Botta. Just off the square are the National School of Music and a university. Interspersed nearby are new office and residential buildings, all constructed of the rich red brick that characterizes the civic and religious edifices of Rights of Man Square.

Responding to this complex site, Kathryn Gustafson conceived a deceptively simple plan. In an effort to distinguish between a plaza for people and the vehicular traffic that surrounds it, Gustafson lowered the center, or heart, of the 1-hectare square. This respite from the surrounding visual and aural turmoil is key to the plaza's autonomy and establishes its distinct, engaging identity.

The open plaza is edged by a double row of small-leafed lime trees on the east side, and pagoda trees, sweet gum, oak, and flowering cherry arranged in series along the north and west borders. Ginkgos line the walkway from the train station to the north. On the east side of the square, a dramatic, 7-meter-high concrete wall, sheathed with sections of mica-sprinkled stone, marks one of two entrances to a parking garage under the square; the other entrance is identified by a grand staircase to the southwest.

It is not, however, the trees, wall, or stair that in any way dominate a visitor's experience of the square. Rather, the plaza's open plan includes a gridded granite floor, a dramatically raised serpentine water basin, a "field" of playful water jets shooting into the air, a rectangular bub-

bling pool, distinctive seating, and a variety of visual and spatial approaches to the imposing architecture surrounding the square that create the dual qualities of respite and dynamism.

Gustafson paved the square in a light-toned Celtic gray granite to highlight the red brick of the surrounding buildings. A grid of white granite on the square gray pavers forms a unifying carpet, accentuating each element with its own horizontal plane, making the surface of the square a series of sloping and complex levels. These varied levels are designed to complement the specific scale, texture, and weight of each building, resulting in a coherent whole.

In front of the cathedral, Gustafson's curving granite staircase to the parking garage below echoes the cathedral's massive scale and the geometry of Botta's round facade. Similarly, the arrangement of the serpentine pool, which Gustafson calls the Dragon Basin, complements the town hall: a pathway leading to the town hall interrupts the pool with a stair, and also serves as the main walkway across the square.

The Dragon Basin, 130 meters long and varying from 5 to 8 meters in width, is the square's most significant visual and artistic gesture. Traversing the southeast

Stone pavers during construction

Dragon Basin joint and horizontal tolerance testing in factory

Dragon Basin with water run at base to collect overflow

Grand staircase during construction

Dragon Basin model

quadrant, the basin's form metamorphosed from a sketch in an early design drawing to a massive river of dark green Brazilian granite. An abstract, organic shape that dominates the otherwise angular space, the basin's mirrorlike surface overflows in sheets along its raised granite sidewalls. One of three water components in the square, the basin's snakelike form creates something intuitively organic against which to measure the human body. The dragon also visually connects the three major buildings—cathedral, chamber of commerce, and town hall—gesturing toward their entrances.

The channel of the basin is composed of 26 pieces of individually cut granite, each 15 centimeters thick and varying from 5 to 8 meters in width and length and 60 centimeters to 2.5 meters above the sloping ground plane of the plaza. Because the stones each have unique angles, they were cut by master stone carvers from Brittany. From Gustafson's clay model, Gérard Pras worked with François Le Manse, who generated a 3D computer model and detailed construction drawings. The walls vary in height according to the inconsistent levels of the plaza floor to create the basin's smooth horizontal surface; the sheer weight of the stones resting on rubber seals forms a waterproofing system.

Gustafson designed places along the edge of the basin to sit, enabling people to run their hands through the water or contemplate reflections on the still surface. The basin also serves as guardrail, eliminating the need for a separate safety fence.

Across the square to the north is the performance area, which Gustafson conceived as a flexible space to accommodate a variety of performances. Major shows or musical entertainment can be mounted on the outdoor theater's rectangular stage, viewed by the audience from tiered seating on its north side. That scenario can be reversed for smaller productions, with performances on the tiers and viewers seated on the granite plaza floor. On the eastern end of the theater, a formed steel guardrail is designed for standing and leaning, designating a standing-room-only balcony.

When no formal event is in the theater, Gustafson offers her own ongoing presentation with a field of water jets emerging from a pattern of holes in the granite south of the tiers. One hundred and fifty-three jets are programmed to send streams of water dancing in the sunlight in varying formats.

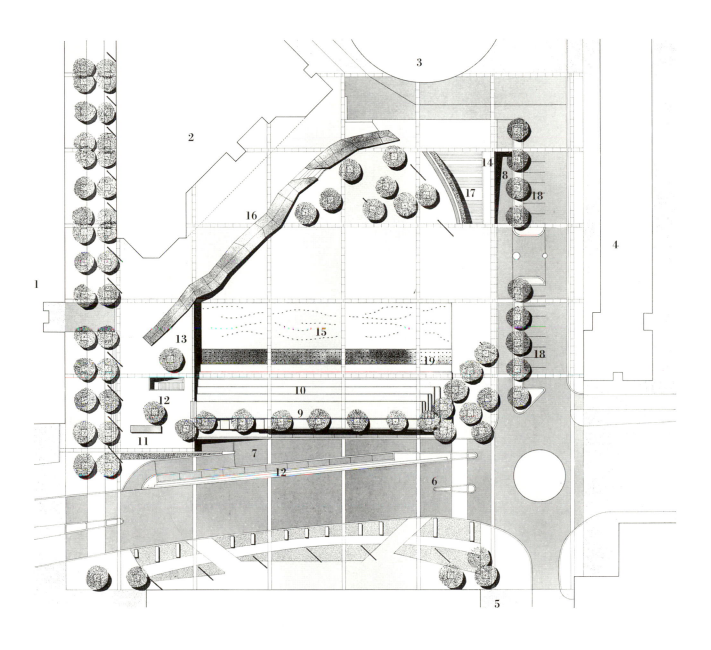

0   50 m ▼

Steel mesh guardrail

Table bench

Simmering Pool and field of water jets, with signal wall in background

Water movement in Simmering Pool

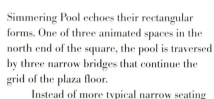
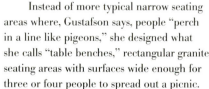

Parking garage below plaza

The 6-millimeter-diameter water jets are thin enough to bend in the wind like grasses, alluding to the agricultural fields that originally occupied the town center. Each stream is orchestrated to perform at differing heights—up to 3 meters—at various times of the day. At night the streams are lit individually, forming a delicate line of light like an ever-changing drawing in space.

The water jets also have an interactive component: as a visitor steps on a jet hole, water spurts out higher from another, although not necessarily from the most obvious or closest one. This feature has been the focus of much good-humored investigation, with adults, children, and even animals venturing to explore the pattern of the system and sometimes getting wet in the process. The jets shoot directly out of the rock, and a return system recycles the water.

To the north of the water jets, the Simmering Pool suggests the activity of lava and other elements churning beneath the earth's veneer. This aerated water fountain makes a bubbling, swirling pattern, stirring the water and air with a continuous turbulence. Sited between the water jets to the south and the performance space to the north, the 50-meter-long, 4-meter-wide

Simmering Pool echoes their rectangular forms. One of three animated spaces in the north end of the square, the pool is traversed by three narrow bridges that continue the grid of the plaza floor.

Instead of more typical narrow seating areas where, Gustafson says, people "perch in a line like pigeons," she designed what she calls "table benches," rectangular granite seating areas with surfaces wide enough for three or four people to spread out a picnic.

The lighting in Rights of Man Square is based on the contrasts of light and shadow. Gustafson has divided and juxtaposed lighting so that all illumination inside the central heart of the plaza, where there are no trees but where the fountains and pools are located, is reflective and indirect, using shadow on structures to reinforce composition and line. Everything surrounding the heart of the square is lit by lamp mounts designed by Gustafson in collaboration with the architectural lighting manufacturer Thorn Europhane. At night, lighting captures the movement of water causing a rippling light show.

The inclined support walls that create the waterfalls along the Dragon Basin are lit by long fluorescent lights positioned under the lip of the channel, which illuminate the

rushing water with a shimmering, mysterious radiance. Each stair contains a light that reflects against its corresponding riser. A play of shadows all along the perimeter of the square from lighting mounted within the tree grates enhances the dramatic effect of the space at night.

Gustafson was careful to integrate the 130-car parking lot beneath the plaza into the spirit of the project. Selecting rich colors and materials that unify underground and surface, she employs natural light and view corridors to emphasize safety, both physically and psychologically. A white granite wall at the connecting stairwell wall forms the corridor that joins the plaza to the underground parking. From the corridor, a 30-centimeter-wide by 20-meter-long eye-level slit in the wall offers views of the water jets and the Simmering Pool and also brings daylight and the sounds of water into the parking area. For safety as well as esthetics, the garage is devoid of large columns or hiding places, and there are no dark spaces.

The main staircase at the plaza's southwest corner protects pedestrians by another custom-designed steel guardrail. The rail also serves as a place to lean and relax, and is designed with a false perspective to enhance the scale of the cathedral and pull a

Formed steel guard rail

Water jets, Simmering Pool, and tiers, viewed through slit in parking access corridor

visitor's eye toward Botta's imposing cylindrical structure. Gustafson treats every design element and functional necessity, no matter how mundane, as an opportunity to create something unexpected: the guardrail, for example, is composed of multilayered stainless steel mesh fastened into a steel frame, creating a moiré effect.

There is no sense of garden at Evry, no flowers, and relatively scant planting, except for the trees and some boxwood hedges near the grand staircase. Since the trees are therefore a particularly important part of Rights of Man Square, the designer required that every tree reach deep into the ground to be rooted in the earth, even if that meant digging down several stories.

With its breadth of venues for performance, Rights of Man Square in the new town of Evry exemplifies the individual and public spirit in its accommodations for communication and interaction. Turning a town plaza into an arena for artistic adventure and playful responses, Gustafson has enlivened the square so that the citizens of Evry can maximize its use for meaningful and memorable expression.

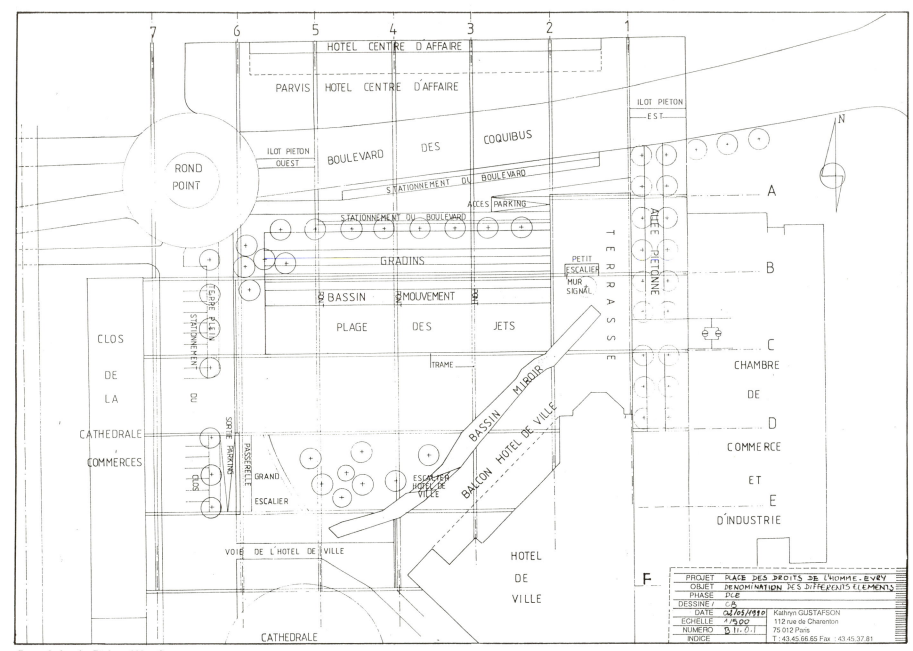

60

General plan for Rights of Man Square

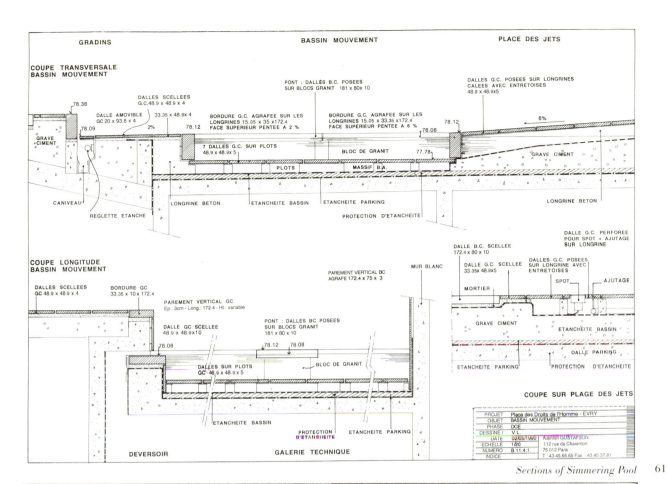

GRADINS   **BASSIN MOUVEMENT**   **PLACE DES JETS**

COUPE TRANSVERSALE
BASSIN MOUVEMENT

PONT : DALLES B.C. POSEES
SUR BLOCS GRANIT 181 x 80x 10

DALLES G.C. POSEES SUR LONGRINES
CALEES AVEC ENTRETOISES
48.9 x 48.9x5

78.38

DALLES SCELLEES
G.C.48.9 x 48.9x 4

DALLE AMOVIBLE
GC 20 x 93.8 x 4

33.35 x 48.9x 4

BORDURE G.C. AGRAFEE SUR LES
LONGRINES 15.05 x 35 x172.4
FACE SUPERIEUR PENTEE A 2 %

BORDURE G.C. AGRAFEE SUR LES
LONGRINES 15.05 x 33.35 x172.4
FACE SUPERIEUR PENTEE A 6 %

6%

78.09
2%
78.12
78.12
78.08
78.12

GRAVE
CIMENT

7 DALLES G.C. SUR PLOTS
48.9 x 48.9 x 5

BLOC DE GRANIT

77.78

GRAVE CIMENT

PLOTS   MASSIF B.A.

CANIVEAU

LONGRINE BETON   ETANCHEITE BASSIN   ETANCHEITE PARKING

LONGRINE BETON

REGLETTE ETANCHE

PROTECTION D'ETANCHEITE

DALLE G.C. PERFOREE
POUR SPOT + AJUTAGE
SUR LONGRINE

COUPE LONGITUDE
BASSIN MOUVEMENT

PAREMENT VERTICAL BC
AGRAFE 172.4 x 75 x 3

MUR BLANC

DALLE B.C. SCELLEE
172.4 x 80 x 10

DALLE G.C. SCELLEE
33.35x 48.9x5

DALLES G.C. POSEES
SUR LONGRINE AVEC
ENTRETOISES

DALLES SCELLEES
GC 48.9 x 48.9 x 4

BORDURE GC
33.35 x 10 x 172.4

PAREMENT VERTICAL GC
Ep.: 3cm - Long.: 172.4 - Ht.: variable

MORTIER

SPOT   AJUTAGE

DALLE GC SCELLEE
48.9 x 48.9x10

PONT : DALLES BC POSEES
SUR BLOCS GRANIT
181 x 80 x 10

78.08
78.12   78.08

GRAVE CIMENT

ETANCHEITE BASSIN

DALLES SUR PLOTS
GC 48.9 x 48.9 x 5

BLOC DE GRANIT

DALLE PARKING

ETANCHEITE PARKING   PROTECTION D'ETANCHEITE

ETANCHEITE BASSIN

PROTECTION
D'ETANCHEITE

ETANCHEITE PARKING

COUPE SUR PLAGE DES JETS

DEVERSOIR   GALERIE TECHNIQUE

PROJET	Place des Droits de l'Homme - EVRY
OBJET	BASSIN MOUVEMENT
PHASE	DCE
DESSINE /	V.L.
DATE	02/05/1990 Kathryn GUSTAFSON
ECHELLE	1/20 112 rue de Charenton
NUMERO	B.11.4.1. 75.012 Paris
INDICE	T : 43.45.66.65 Fax : 43.45.37.81

Sections of Simmering Pool   61

COUPE

DALLE GRANIT Vert Tropical - Epaisseur 15cm

COUPE BISEAU FORMANT BANC

BISSECTRICE

50   165   165   65   27   15

NIV. EAU

80.85   80.82   80.81

80.44

80.55   80.47

3   52   8

Parement agrafé
en granit Vert Tropical
Epaisseur 3cm

Béton léger

80.00

DALLE PARKING

Dalle granit
Gris celtique
48.9 x 48.9

Recueil des eaux de fuite

Règlette
lumineuse
étanche

Caniveau à grille

Barbacane au droit des joints
des dalles formant bassin

Equerre INOX

Béton léger

Caniveau

ELEVATION

80.85

DALLE GRANIT
Vert tropical - Epaisseur 15cm
CHANTS VERTICAUX

80.45

PAREMENT Vert Tropical
GRANIT - Epaisseur 3cm

DALLAGE GRANIT
Gris Celtique 48.9 x 48.9

43   27   43   33   54   54   24   33   54

PROJET	Place des Droits de l'Homme - EVRY
OBJET	BASSIN MIROIR - COUPE ELEVATION
PHASE	DCE
DESSINE /	G.P.
DATE	02/05/1990 Kathryn GUSTAFSON
ECHELLE	1/20 112 rue de Charenton
NUMERO	B.11.5.2. 75.012 Paris
INDICE	T : 43.45.66.65 Fax : 43.45.37.81

Section and elevation of Dragon Basin, supporting wall, and water run

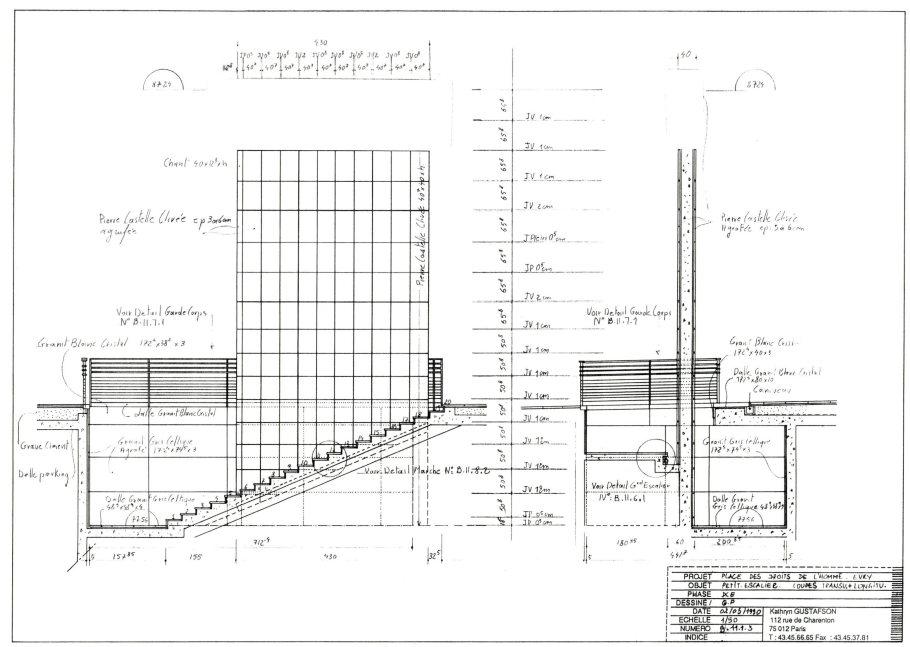

62

Sections of signal wall denoting pedestrian entrance to parking garage

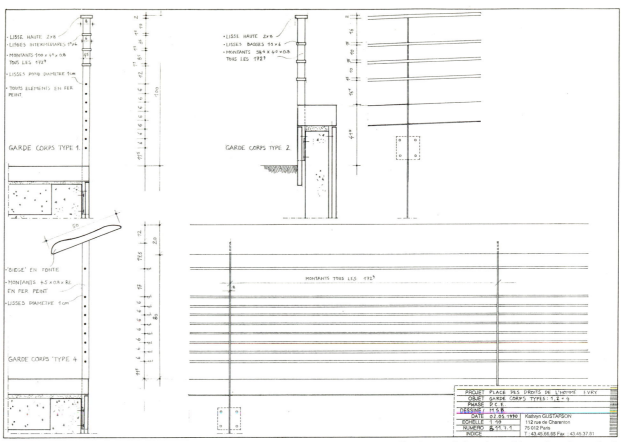

Sections and elevations of formed steel guardrail

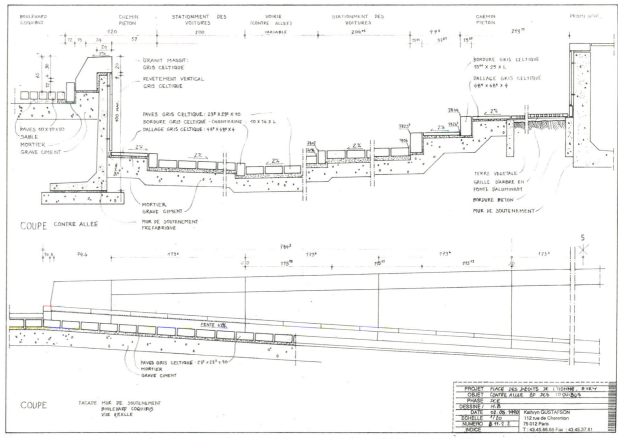

Section and elevation of parking vehicle entry and walkway to balcony and promenade

64 **Notes**

1 Simon Schama, *Landscape and Memory*
(New York: Alfred A. Knopf, 1995, pg. 61).

2 Susan L. Stoops, ed. *More than
Minimal: Feminism and Abstraction in
the '70s* (Waltham, MA: Brandeis
University, 1996).

3 Dorothée Imbert, *The Modernist Garden
in France* (New Haven, CT: Yale
University Press, 1993).

Bibliography

Armstrong, Richard, and Richard Marshall,
eds. *The New Sculpture 1965–75:
Between Geometry and Gesture.*
Catalogue to exhibition at Whitney
Museum of American Art. New York:
Whitney Museum of American Art,
1990.

Beardsley, John. *Earthworks and Beyond.*
New York: Abbeville, 1989.

Garraud, Colette. *L'idée de nature dans
l'art contemporain.* Paris: Flammarion,
1994.

Imbert, Dorothée. *The Modernist Garden
in France.* New Haven, CT: Yale
University Press, 1993.

Kemal, Salim, and Ivan Gaskell, eds.
*Landscape, Natural Beauty and the
Arts.* Cambridge, England: Cambridge
University Press, 1993.

Lippard, Lucy. Overlay: *Contemporary Art
and the Art of Prehistory.* New York:
Pantheon Books, 1983.

Rubin, William, ed. *Primitivism in 20th
Century Art, Affinity of the Tribal and
the Modern,* Vol. 2, especially Kirk
Varnedoe, "Contemporary Explora-
tions." Catalogue to exhibition at the
Museum of Modern Art, New York.
Boston: Little, Brown, 1984.

Stoops, Susan L., ed. *More than Minimal:
Feminism and Abstraction in the '70s.*
Catalogue to exhibition at Brandeis
University. Waltham, MA: Brandeis
University, 1996.

Streep, Peg. *Sanctuaries of the Goddess:
The Sacred Landscapes and Objects.*
Boston: Little, Brown, 1994.

Weilacher, Udo. *Between Landscape
Architecture and Land Art.* Basel:
Kirkhauser Verlag, 1996.

Photography
Photography by Luc Boegly except
as noted and:

Page 9, aerial photographs, © Amyn

Pages 21, 22-23, 29, 36, 37, 40, 41 by
Kathryn Gustafson